100 FACTS YOU SHOULD KNOW

MAGIC AND MYSTERY

Carey Scott

Consultant: Fiona Macdonald

Gareth Stevens
PUBLISHING

Please visit our website, www.garethstevens.com.
For a free color catalog of all our high-quality books,
call toll free 1-800-542-2595 or fax 1-877-542-2596.

Cataloging-in-Publication Data

Names: Scott, Carey. | Macdonald, Fiona, consultant.
Title: Magic and Mystery / Carey Scott; consultant, Fiona Macdonald.
Description: New York : Gareth Stevens Publishing, 2016. | Series: 100 facts you should know | Includes index.
Identifiers: ISBN 9781482451405 (pbk.) | ISBN 9781482451344 (library bound) | ISBN 9781482451221 (6 pack)
Subjects: LCSH: Magic--Juvenile literature.
Classification: LCC BF1611.S385 2016 | DDC 133.4'3--dc23

Published in 2017 by
Gareth Stevens Publishing
111 East 14th Street, Suite 349
New York, NY 10003

Copyright © 2017 Miles Kelly Publishing Ltd.

Publishing Director: Belinda Gallagher
Creative Director: Jo Cowan
Assistant Editor: Carly Blake
Volume Designer: Sally Lace
Image Manager: Lorraine King
Indexer: Jane Parker
Production Manager: Elizabeth Collins
Reprographics: Ian Paulyn, Thom Allaway
Assets: Lorraine King

Acknowledgements:

The publishers would like to thank the following artists who have contributed to this book: Mike Foster, Andrea Morandi, Mike White

Cover artwork: Mike White

All other artwork from the Miles Kelly Artwork Bank

The publishers would like to thank the following sources for the use of their photographs: Page 6 © New Line Cinema /Everett/Rex Features; 8(b) National Geographic/Getty Images; 9 Action Press/Rex Features; 10(c) Science Photo Library; 11(t) © Hulton-Deutsch Collection/Corbis, (b) Getty Images; 12 New Line Cinema/The Kobal Collection; 13(t) © The Print Collector/Alamy, (b) © Dover Pictorial Archive; 17 © sharply_done/Fotolia.com; 20 Rex Features; 22(t) John Hooper/Hoopix®/MoW, (b) © Mikhail Lukyanov/Fotolia.com; 23 © Lindsay Hebberd/Corbis; 24–25 Getty Images; 24(b) © prints2buy/Fotolia.com; 25 © Jgz/Fotolia.com; 27 Bob Langrish; 28(b) © Alison Wright/ Corbis, (t) © Uros Petrovic/Fotolia.com; 31(t) © Elena Butinova/Fotolia.com, (c) © Maksym 32 © Sebastian Kaulitzki/Fotolia.com, (t) John Hooper/Hoopix®/MoW; 33(b) © New Line Cinema/Everett/Rex Features; 35(t) The Granger Collection/Topfoto/TopFoto.co.uk; 37(t) © Mary Evans Picture Library/Alamy, (b) © Warner Brothers/Photos 12/Alamy; 38 (background) © laxmi/Fotolia.com, (b) © Warner Brothers/Photos 12/Alamy; 39(b) © Universal Pictures/Photos 12/Alamy; 40 © Walt Disney Pictures/Topfoto/TopFoto.co.uk; 41(t) © PoodlesRock/ Corbis; 42(b) NMeM/Science & Society; 43(c) © Bettmann/Corbis, (b) Quilici/Iverson/Rex Features; 44–45 © scol22/Fotolia.com; 45 © Robbie Jack/Corbis, (t) © dmitry_kim/Fotolia.com; 46(t) Dimitris Legakis/Rex Features, (c) © Anyka/Fotolia.com, (b) ©1999 Credit:Topham Picturepoint/TopFoto.co.uk; 47 Erik Pendzich/Rex Features

All other photographs are from: Corel, digitalSTOCK, digitalvision, Fotolia.com, iStockphoto.com, John Foxx, PhotoAlto, PhotoDisc, PhotoEssentials, PhotoPro, Stockbyte

Printed in the United States of America

CPSIA compliance information: Batch CS16GS: For further information contact Gareth Stevens, New York, New York at 1-800-542-2595.

Contents

What is magic?

1 **Throughout history and all over the world, people have believed in magic.** The word "magic" describes powers or events that are beyond scientific understanding. Belief in magic probably began as a way of explaining seemingly mysterious events, such as earthquakes, disease, or a run of good luck. Magic has always formed a part of religious beliefs, for example, as supernatural beings called gods. Different magical ideas are also found in the popular beliefs and traditions of a culture, called folklore.

▲ J. R. R. Tolkien's fantasy novel *The Lord of the Rings* (1954) is one of the most popular magical stories ever written. This scene from the 2002 film *The Lord of the Rings: The Two Towers* shows the good wizard Gandalf the White returning to meet his friends.

History of magic

2 **It is likely that belief in magic originated in prehistoric times.** Cave paintings in Europe and North Africa depict scenes that may show magical rituals. By around 5,000 years ago, when people began recording their beliefs in writing, magic was part of their lives.

3 **In ancient civilizations such as Greece and Rome, magic was a part of everyday life.** Most people believed that invisible beings existed, that the future could be predicted and that magical events occurred.

▼ In the 1600s, Isaac Newton began to dispel magical beliefs by showing that rainbows were made by sunlight being scattered into many colors by water drops, or glass.

▲ This drawing of a 10,000-year-old cave painting in France may show a figure performing a magical dance.

4 **During the medieval period (500–1450), and up to about 1700, most Europeans believed in witchcraft.** Some scientists and scholars practiced magic along with sciences such as mathematics. Yet by around 1800, developments in chemistry and physics were able to explain many events and natural phenomena once thought to be magical, such as rainbows.

5 **In the modern world, magic has lost much of its power, but it has not disappeared.** Fortune-telling, especially astrology, is still popular. Magical healing lives on in some alternative medicines. Yet for most people, the word "magic" means tricks of illusion performed by stage magicians rather than supernatural powers.

▲ A popular stage magic trick is to create the illusion of levitation – a person rising into the air without any visible support.

6 **In traditional beliefs in some parts of the world, magic still survives today.** Among native North Americans and in parts of Asia and Africa, shamans, (spiritual healers) carry out traditional healing in their local communities. Magicians and witches can be found even in urban places, such as the cities of Brazil and South Africa.

Magical practices

7 The three main types of magical practice are divination, magic spells, and high magic. Divination is the use of magic to predict the future or discover knowledge. Magic spells are used to achieve specific results. High magic aims to gain control over nature through magical knowledge.

8 Astrology is a well known form of divination. Astrologists believe that the positions of the Sun, Moon, stars and planets influence peoples' lives, and can be used to predict the future. Astrology began in the ancient world and spread to many different countries.

Love spell

On Midsummer's Eve, pick a red rose and wrap it in white silk. Hide it away in a safe place until Christmas. Then open the silk and if the flower is still intact, wear it on your person. The first person to admire it will fall in love with you.

▲ People have used spells to make others fall in love with them for thousands of years, such as this simple white (good) magic love spell.

9 Magic spells aim to help someone achieve a particular result. A spell may be intended to heal or harm a person, or make them fall in love. It may also give protection against harmful magic. Often magic spells are passed on by word of mouth, but they have also been written down.

10

Those who practice high magic aim to understand and control the world.
Magicians of 15th- and 16th-century Europe spent years reading ancient books on magic, attending meetings on the subject and taking part in magic rituals. They believed that magic was the key to understanding the secrets of nature, and that mastering it would make them as powerful as gods.

▲ Italian philosopher Giovanni Pico della Mirandola (1463–1494) became interested in high magic after studying ancient magical texts.

◄ This 17th-century illustration shows an astrologer casting someone's horoscope. A personal horoscope might list auspicious (lucky) days.

11

Magic makers have different names.
Shamans use magic to cure illness, but they make spells and practice high magic too. Diviners practice various kinds of divination. Witches cast magic spells, and magicians are interested in high magic.

◄ Diviners called "dowsers" search for water using metal or wooden rods, or pendulums. In Tehuacán, Mexico, a farmer claims he has developed a water-divining method using just a rock dangling from a thin rope.

QUIZ

1. What are the three magical practices?
2. How do astrologists predict the future?
3. Who practices high magic?

Answers:
1. Divination, magic spells, high magic 2. By studying the positions of the Sun, Moon, stars and planets 3. Magicians and shamans

People with magical powers

In many cultures throughout history, some people have been seen as magical. Often they were admired and respected. However, if it was thought that a magic maker was practicing harmful magic, they might be severely punished.

▲ In the film *The Golden Compass* (2007), people's souls are animal-like spirits called daemons. Like the daemons of ancient Greeks, they can give advice to their human companions.

In ancient Greece, people were thought to have access to magical beings.

Socrates (469–399 BC)

They believed that everyone had a protecting magical spirit, called a daemon, which accompanied them through life. The most well-known daemon belonged to Socrates and it was thought to advise its master against doing anything dangerous.

I DON'T BELIEVE IT!

In Europe, between 1400–1650, elderly women living alone, especially those with pets, were likely to be accused of being witches.

14

In ancient and modern times, rulers have been seen as magical. In ancient Egypt, people thought the pharaoh had so much power he could make the earth tremble by raising his hand. Until 1945, emperors of Japan were seen as living gods descended from the Sun goddess Amaterasu. In some religious beliefs, rulers are closer to gods than ordinary people.

▶ Emperor Hirohito, shown here in his coronation robes, rejected his divine status after Japan's defeat in World War II (1939–1945).

15

In Europe, for more than 200 years, people were executed if they were thought to be witches. Many thousands of people were hanged, drowned, or burned for practicing harmful magic. Some experts think witchcraft was invented to persecute people who did not fit into society.

▲ One reason shamans wear costumes is to emphasize their powers when conducting rituals and ceremonies.

▼ In 1612, during the Lancashire witch trials in England, ten people were found guilty of murder by witchcraft and hanged.

16

Only people thought to have magical powers can be shamans. As well as being able to see into the future, shamans communicate with spirits, which enables them to be healers. Shamans gain their powers through a natural "calling," or through experiences, such as illness.

Alchemy

17 Alchemy was a scientific and magical art, which aimed to change common metals into gold. It was first practiced in the ancient world. Ancient Greek philosopher Aristotle taught that all matter was made up of four elements, and altering their amounts could change one substance into another.

Cauldron

19 Alchemists did not want to make gold to become rich. They saw gold as the most perfect, pure substance. Having the ability to turn ordinary metals, such as lead, into pure gold was thought to have a similar effect on the alchemist – he would be turned into a higher being.

Glass still

18 The alchemist's main aim was to find the Philosopher's Stone. Alchemists thought that only this magical substance could change metal into gold. An elixir made from the stone was also thought to grant eternal life. But the alchemists searched in vain.

Bellows

Animal skull

▼ An alchemist's laboratory was often hidden away in the cellar or attic of his home, and would have been cluttered with equipment to carry out experiments.

20 When magic failed, alchemists used trickery. Their most common trick was to conceal gold in the stick they used to stir the molten metal, so it looked as though gold was being produced.

Alchemical textbook

21 Alchemists made major scientific breakthroughs. They found ways of refining metals, and first described important substances such as hydrochloric acid and arsenic. They made their discoveries by carrying out experiments in laboratories, just as chemists do today.

Pestle and mortar

Dishes of dried plants and powdered substances

Making predictions

22 There are over 50 ways of predicting, or divining, the future. Some divination methods look for signs of warning or guidance to help with making decisions and answering questions. Other methods include fortune-telling, which tries to discover an individual's future.

▼ The most important oracle in ancient Greece was at Delphi. The priestess at the temple of Apollo would go into a trance. The god then spoke through her, giving magical words of advice.

23 The ancient Greeks used divination to help them make important decisions. If a general was thinking about going to war or considering marriage, he consulted an oracle. This was a place where a priestess in a temple was thought to be able to see the future by communicating with the temple god.

▶ Ancient Chinese diviners recorded their predictions on bones in an early form of Chinese writing.

▶ Telling the future by studying the flight patterns and cries of birds is called augury.

24 More than 3,000 years ago, the Shang kings of ancient China relied on a method of divination that used animal bones. The king went to see a diviner with a particular question. The diviner inscribed the question on the bone and then heated it until the bone cracked. The answer to the king's question was "read" from the cracks formed by the heat.

25 Tasseographers see a person's future in the patterns in tea leaves or coffee grounds. Tea-leaf reading started in the ancient world. A tasseographer looks for certain shapes in the tea leaves, which mean particular things. Seeing the shape of a house means change and success, but a mountain foresees obstruction.

▶ In palmistry, the most prominent four lines on the hand are called the heart line, head line, life line, and fate line. The right hand is read unless the person is left-handed.

PALM LINES
1. **Life line** Length and vitality of a person's life
2. **Head line** Mentality and intelligence
3. **Heart line** Emotions
4. **Fate line** Fortune and success

26 Palm reading is the art of reading a person's character and future from the lines on their hands. It was first practiced over 5,000 years ago in India. In the 1900s, a palm-reading craze swept the US and Britain, and palm readers read the hands of the British royal family and Hollywood stars.

27 **What is a magic spell?** It is a set of words to be spoken or chanted, often during a ritual of some kind. If the magic spell is directed at a particular person, then using their name, or having a personal possession or a picture of them is thought to increase the power of it.

28 In medieval England, written spells were thought to be especially effective magic, probably because few people could write. In Cornwall, white witches called "pellars" sold written spells as protection against harmful magic. For best results, pellars recommended placing their spells under a pillow.

29 In mainland Europe, from the 18th to 20th centuries, people performed a ceremony to keep witches away. On May Eve (April 30th) people ran around their houses and villages seven times, shouting "Witch flee, flee from here, or it will go ill with thee." In Germany, May Eve was a day for burning witches at the stake.

30 In Mexico, the Day of the Dead is celebrated in November. Ceremonies are held to encourage the souls of dead people to visit the living. People make offerings to the dead, including sugar skulls and sweets. The souls of the dead are said to consume the sweets' spiritual essence.

▶ This typical Day of the Dead altar is crowded with intricately decorated sugar skulls. The skeletons represent dead loved ones.

17

Helpful magic

▶ A Native American Indian performs a rain dance at a reservoir in Derbyshire, England, during a drought in 1995. Science has been unable to make rain, so people still occasionally put their faith in magic instead.

31 Ceremonies, spells, and magic potions have all been used to try to ensure good fortune. Most helpful magic tries to encourage events that may happen anyway. But sometimes people have used magic to try to achieve things that exist only in their dreams, such as immortality.

32 From ancient Egypt to 21st-century North America, people have performed magic ceremonies in the hope of bringing rain. In May 2008, after a long drought in Georgia, Native Americans from the Shoshone, Cherokee and Muscogee nations gathered at a sacred site and performed a ceremony to bring rain.

33 **Magic has been used to make a person fall in love.** An example from a 10th-century Arabic book on magic called *Picatrix* suggested putting two dolls in a fireplace and a piece of ice in the fire. When the ice melted, the lovers' hearts would supposedly melt too. This is imitative magic – it hopes to influence events by imitating them.

▲ Witchetty grubs are a useful source of protein for some indigenous Australian peoples.

34 **In some cultures, magic is used to ensure a good supply of food.** Indigenous peoples of central Australia eat an insect lava called a witchetty grub. They perform a ceremony that mimics the grub emerging from its chrysalis, to ensure there will be plenty of them to eat. In Mauritius, fishermen attach pictures of fish to trees on the beach to help them make a big catch.

35 **Some magicians believed eternal life was possible.** In medieval Europe, magicians thought that a potion called the Elixir of Life could grant the drinker eternal life. In ancient China, magician Wei Po-Yang claimed he had created a Pill of Immortality. The secret of eternal life is still looked for today – in science.

▼ Ouroboros – a dragon forming a circle by swallowing its own tail – is an ancient symbol of immortality.

19

Harmful magic

36 The idea of using a doll to magically harm a person has been known in cultures around the world. A magical link is thought to exist between the doll and the person it represents, so harming the doll harms the person too. Dolls were stuck with pins, but might also have been burned or boiled.

▼ In medieval European folklore, a person's shadow represented their soul. People who had sold their souls to the devil were thought to cast no shadow.

▲ This clay puppet doll from Cornwall, England, has had rows of small nails driven into its chest. This would have been intended to harm the person it represented.

37 It was thought that harming a person's shadow could harm the person too. In the 19th century, magicians of the island of Wetar, Indonesia, were said to be able to cause illness by stabbing a person's shadow. Into the 20th century, in parts of Central Africa and India, folklore said that spearing a person's shadow could kill them.

38 In medieval Europe, textbooks of magic began to appear. The books were called "grimoires" and were written by magicians. They contained instructions for calling up and commanding supernatural beings that would carry out the magician's orders. Complicated ceremonies to summon up the beings were described in detail.

QUIZ

1. What were medieval magic textbooks called?
2. Who is born with magical powers — sorcerers or witches?
3. What is *ojo* commonly known as?

Answers:
1. Grimoires 2. Witches 3. The "evil eye".

39 In some traditional African communities, sorcerers and witches use different forms of harmful magic. Sorcerers carry out magic with potions and magical objects and they learn magic from other sorcerers. Witches are born with magical powers and they can cause harm to someone just by concentrating bad feeling on them.

▶ In ancient Rome, people asked the gods to harm their enemies. They would leave a tablet inscribed with their foe's name and curse words at a temple.

40 Mexican folklore says that *ojo*, or "evil eye," is a major cause of childhood illness. Today, some Mexicans still believe that common illnesses can be caused by an intense stare. A witch can deliberately cause *ojo*, but a person with very strong vision could also create *ojo* by accident.

▼ The Bhil people of India think that evil spirits cause illness. The black powder around this baby's eyes is to protect her against the "evil eye."

21

41 Glastonbury Tor in England is believed to be a center of mystical energy. The natural, cone-shaped hill has flattened steps, called terraces, shaped into it, which may be the remains of a maze used for religious rituals. The site is also said to be crisscrossed by tracks of magical energy called ley lines.

◄ The stone circle at Callanish on the Scottish island of Lewis. According to folklore the stones were once living giants, who were turned to stone.

42 In many parts of the world, early peoples built stone circles from boulders. Some historians think they were sacred burial grounds, or temples where magic may have been carried out. Another theory suggests that they helped people observe and map the movements of the Sun, Moon, and stars.

43 For native Australian peoples, a sandstone mass is the most magical place on Earth. Uluru rises out of the central Australian desert and is thought to be crossed by magical "dreaming tracks." According to traditional belief, spirit ancestors created the tracks as they traveled the land, singing the world into existence.

▼ Glastonbury Tor is a natural hill that is 492 feet (150m) high. its top is St. Michael's Tower, the remains of a medieval church.

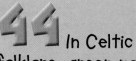

44 In Celtic folklore, green mounds are entrances to the underworld. Magical beings lived in the underworld and Celtic people thought these beings could emerge from grassy mounds and interact with humans. It was thought that humans might be able to enter the underworld there too.

▶ A spider so big it can be seen fully only from the air is one of the animal drawings of the Nazca lines.

◀ The lone mountain of Uluru, also called Ayers Rock, is almost 1,148 feet (350m) high and measures 5.84 miles (9.4km) in circumference.

45 High on a desert-like plain in Peru, South America, lies one of the great mysteries of the world. Covering an incredible 193 square miles (500 sq m) are hundreds of huge drawings of animals and plants, carved into the ground. The Nazca Lines, as they are known, were made around 2,000 years ago. Some historians think they were made for gods in the sky to see. Others think the drawings were a kind of cosmic calendar.

Animal magic

46 In folklore, real and mythical animals can have magical powers. Animals may be good – folktales from around the world tell of birds that give warnings or advice to humans. But they can also be evil, such as the dragon that terrorizes a town in the legend of Saint George and the Dragon.

47 Dragons are believed to control the forces of nature. In ancient Chinese folklore, these mythical animals are responsible for the running of the world. The Terrestrial Dragon looks after streams and rivers and can cause floods and droughts. The Divine Dragon controls winds and rain, and makes lightning by flashing its eyes.

▲ Legend says George killed the dragon that terrorized the people of Lydia (in modern Turkey).

▲ In Chinese mythology, dragons are helpful. Each Chinese New Year, dragon dances are performed to scare off evil spirits.

▶ Black cats are most commonly depicted as witches' familiars.

48 Animals could be witches' helpers. In medieval Europe, some people believed that spirits could live in animals' bodies. Called "familiars," these animals could be witches' servants and companions. Frogs, snakes and spiders have been depicted as witches' familiars, as well as cats.

In ancient Egypt, causing the death of a cat was a serious crime. When one Roman soldier accidentally killed one, he was himself killed by a furious mob.

49 Animals were thought to be able to foresee death. Gaelic folklore tells that in 597 BC, Saint Columba sat down to rest, and a horse came up to him. Sensing that he was dying, it laid its head on his chest and cried. Saint Columba died soon after. A 16th-century English belief says that a dog scratching the floor and howling means that someone nearby is about to die.

▶ The unicorn was imagined as a beautiful, dignified animal with a gentle nature.

50 The unicorn was a mythical horse–like animal with a horn on its forehead. Up until the 1700s, most Europeans believed the unicorn was real, but so shy and fast that it was impossible to catch. According to an ancient Greek text dating from the second century AD, a unicorn would calmly lie down and put its head in the lap of a beautiful young girl.

Healers and healing

51 Shamans of central and north Asia are thought to be able to cure illness by going into a trance and "leaving" their bodies. They believe that disease is caused by a person's soul having been lost or stolen. The shaman's main task in healing is to find and capture the missing soul and return it to the patient's body.

▼ In Nepal, Asia, the Dami Jankris are shamans who carry out traditional healing. Dancing, chanting, and drumming are used during healing ceremonies.

▶ All over the world, healers would be expected to know how to treat illnesses using simple herbs and other plants.

Dandelion leaves and root
Useful for treating liver complaints

52 In England, between the 16th and 20th centuries, villagers called Cunning Folk performed healing using herbs and spells. Cunning Folk knew enough about medicinal herbs to be effective healers. As well as curing illness, it was believed that their healing offered protection against witchcraft.

Never attempt to eat any of the plants mentioned in this book. They could seriously harm you.

Poppy seeds
Used to treat skin complaints, insomnia, and to reduce inflammation

Mint leaves
Used to treat sickness and aid digestion

QUIZ
1. What does a shaman aim to do during healing?
2. What were England's village healers known as?
3. Which ancient Greek god was responsible for healing?

Answers:
1. Find the patient's soul and return it to their body 2. The Cunning Folk 3. Asklepios

53 In ancient Greece, it was believed that remedies for illnesses were revealed in dreams. Believers spent a night at the temple of Asklepios, the god of healing. As they slept, the god entered their dreams with suggestions of remedies. After each successful cure, the details of the illness and the treatment were written down, or carved on the temple walls to record them.

▶ The long tusks of the narwhal were commonly passed off as unicorn horns.

54 Some magical healing was thought to carry an illness away. Ancient Greek philosopher Democritus said that a person stung by a scorpion should sit on a donkey and whisper to it "a scorpion has stung me" to transfer the pain to the animal. In medieval England, a patient was rubbed with an eggshell stuffed with horsehair. This was then thrown into the street to transfer the illness to whoever stepped on it.

55 It was believed that a unicorn's horn could neutralize snakebites, cure the plague, and heal injuries. Horns that were thought to have been taken from unicorns were incredibly valuable. In 1553, a horn owned by the King of France was valued at £20,000 – $7.61 million today. But the King was deceived, for the horn probably came from a rhinoceros, or was the tusk of a narwhal, a type of whale.

Prized plants

Liverwort
Like the human liver, the leaves of liverwort have three lobes, so it was used for treating liver complaints

Walnuts
They look like brains — a sign they may be able to cure headaches

Bloodroot
The root contains red sap, so was used to treat blood ailments (even though it is dangerously poisonous)

56 **Plants held clues to their medicinal uses.** In the 1600s, the book *The Doctrine of Signatures* popularized the idea that God created every plant with a medicinal use. If people could read the signs of those uses, they would see which plants could treat which illnesses.

◀ According to author Jakob Böhme, a plant that resembles a part of the body could be used to treat disorders of that part. Names of many plants reflect this idea.

Lungwort
With spotty leaves that were thought to resemble infected lungs, this plant was used in the treatment of lung disorders

57 **Celtic priests called druids cut mistletoe in a special way to retain its magic.** A druid dressed in white robes cut the plant on the sixth day of the Moon's cycle using a gold sickle. He let it fall onto a white robe and placed the plant in water. The water could then be sprinkled around an area to protect it from evil.

Maidenhair fern
This plant looks as though it could encourage a healthy head of hair

◄ In Scottish folklore, touching someone suspected of being a witch with a rowan branch would ensure that the devil took them away.

YOU DON'T BELIEVE IT!

One traditional English love potion was a mixture of powdered periwinkle flowers and earthworms.

58 The rowan tree, or mountain ash, was thought to protect against harmful magic.

In Celtic Europe, planting rowan trees around a house, or nailing a rowan branch over the door was thought to stop evil spirits from entering. Around 600 years ago, Viking sailors carried rowan-wood amulets for protection against the hostile Norse goddess of the sea, Ran.

◄ Today, mistletoe is used as a Christmas decoration as its pretty (but poisonous) white berries appear in winter.

59 All over the world, people have eaten mushrooms in magic rituals.

Chemicals in some mushrooms are "hallucinogenic." This means that they affect a person's sense of reality, often causing colorful visions. Some magicians think that these effects help people to enter magical worlds.

60 According to legend, the root of the mandrake plant uttered a deadly shriek when it was pulled from the ground.

To avoid being killed by the shriek, people made their dogs dig up the roots. Mandrake root was used in medieval magic rituals, as well as in medicine in central and southern Europe, where it grows natively.

◄ The mandrake root can look like an animal's body, and this one has been carved with the face of a monkey to emphasize the resemblance.

29

Tools, amulets and charms

61 **The wand was a tool for aiming magic at a particular object.** To ensure that a wand had magical qualities, it was supposed to be made of hazelwood cut from the tree at sunrise. A wand for harmful magic was supposed to be cut from a cypress tree at midnight.

▼ Wands were used by witches and magicians in all sorts of magical activities, such as transforming an animal or person into something else.

62 **Amulets were thought to provide magical protection.** They were usually small, carved objects of gods that were carried, or worn in jewelry. Some amulets protected against the "evil eye," others helped women in childbirth and some protected specific parts of the body against injury.

▲ The ancient Romans gave a gold good luck charm called a bulla to their babies.

▶ The ancient Egyptian Eye of Horus was worn for protection and safety.

MAKE A MAGIC AMULET

You will need:
• stiff card • scissors • felt-tip pen

1. Along the long edge of the card write the word ABRACADABRA, leaving space between each letter.
2. Underneath, starting just inside the first A, write ABRACADABR.
3. Carry on, each time leaving off another letter at the end, until your last word is the letter A.
4. You should now have a cone shape of magic letters. Cut it out and put it up it in a special place. In medieval times, the Abracadabra amulet was thought to protect against disease.

```
A B R A C A D A B R A
 A B R A C A D A B R
  A B R A C A D A B
   A B R A C A D A
    A B R A C A D
     A B R A C A
      A B R A C
       A B R A
        A B R
         A B
          A
```

◀ This amulet was carried by Viking warriors for strength.

63 A horseshoe nailed to a door was believed to keep out evil spirits and witches. Iron horseshoes are lucky charms in all countries where horses are used. This is probably because blacksmiths are associated with magic. According to ancient folklore, they were taught metalworking by magical beings.

64 In 16th-century England, many people thought rings could have magical properties. Inscriptions were believed to increase their magical properties – people wore rings inscribed with names of holy people to keep the plague and other illnesses away. The influential and successful Cardinal Wolsey was accused of bewitching King Henry VIII by giving him a magical ring.

◀ Even today, people nail horseshoes to their front doors to bring them good luck.

▶ Frodo reaches for The One Ring in the film *The Lord of the Rings: The Fellowship of the Ring* (2001). The magical ring makes the wearer invisible and forces him to enter a spirit world.

Symbols

65 **In ancient Egypt, hieroglyphs (picture symbols) were thought to possess the power of the beings they depicted.** Sculptors were nervous of carving a complete animal inside a tomb in case it came alive. A hieroglyph of a demon was always cut through the centre to stop it having any evil influence.

66 **A pentagram – a star with five points – has been used in magic rituals.** The symbol was thought to be important in bringing good magical influences. For medieval magicians, the five points represented the four elements – earth, air, fire, and water – and the spiritual essence of life, called quintessence.

▶ The right way up, the pentagram was used in helpful magic, but upside down it became a symbol of evil.

Pentagram

67 **Symbols backwards or upside down were associated with harmful magic.** Such symbols suggested choosing evil over good. An upside-down cross was a sign of devil worship, and an upside-down pentagram symbolized evil because it overturned the accepted order of things.

I DON'T BELIEVE IT!

The symbols on rune stones are the letters of an ancient alphabet. Each letter was thought to possess magical power. Today, some people use rune stones in a form of divination.

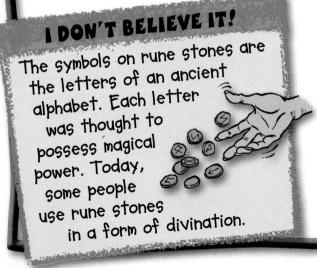

◀ The mythical magician, Dr. Faustus, who sold his soul to the devil. The magic circle he stands in is ringed with symbols to protect him from the evil spirits he is conjuring up.

69 **A circle was also an important symbol in high magic rituals.** During these rituals, the magician and his assistant stayed inside the circle, believing this would contain and concentrate their magical energy. It was also thought this would protect them from the spirits or powerful forces they might summon up.

68 **The circle is thought to be a protective magical symbol because it is without a beginning or end.** Around 1000 BC in Babylon (now Iraq), a circle of flour drawn around a sick person was thought to keep demons away. Similarly, a Jewish custom in medieval Germany recommended drawing a circle around the bed of a woman in childbirth to ensure a safe birth.

▼ Hex signs decorate barns in an area of Pennsylvania called Pennsylvania Dutch Country.

Hex sign

70 **In Pennsylvania, barns are painted with colorful "hex signs."** The signs are thought to protect animals and crops against harmful magic. The tradition was brought over by German settlers hundreds of years ago, and it still lives on today as a form of folk art. The first hex signs were six-sided stars, but now there are many different designs.

Famous magic makers

71 **The most famous magician is Merlin.** Legendary advisor to British King Arthur, Merlin's powers included the ability to see the future. Legend says that Merlin used magic to arrange Arthur's birth and then to make sure he became king, because he knew Arthur would be a great ruler.

▼ Merlin as we recognize him today made his first appearance in stories by Geoffrey of Monmouth, written in the 12th century.

72 **Russian and East European folklore tells of a witch called Baba Yaga.** The old woman lives in a hut perched on giant chicken's feet. She flies through the air with a giant pestle and mortar, and kidnaps and cooks children in her enormous oven.

73 **Simon Magus, or Simon the Sorcerer, lived in the first century AD.** People believed he could fly, become invisible, appear as an animal – and even that he was a demon in disguise. This was probably because he went against accepted beliefs to start his own religion.

◀ Scholar John Dee (1527–1608) wrote several books about magic that he claimed were told to him by angels.

74 Scientist and mathematician John Dee was the most important magician of 16th-century England. As a young man he became an advisor to Queen Elizabeth I – he read her horoscope and used astrology to decide the day of her coronation. Later, he became interested in magic to gain knowledge about the secrets of life and nature.

75 In 13th-century Germany, scholar and magician Albertus Magnus was reported to have built a magical metal head that could answer any question. Magnus studied subjects including alchemy and astrology, and was so clever that people thought he must be capable of magical feats. However, the magical head was never found.

▶ In the film *Harry Potter and the Order of the Phoenix* (2007), Harry uses his magical powers to battle the evil Lord Voldemort.

76 In modern times, magic-making lives on in J. K. Rowling's boy-wizard, Harry Potter. Among his magical powers are the ability to fly on a broomstick, conjure up objects, transport himself from one place to another and read people's minds. Harry uses his powers to battle against evil.

Mischievous magic

77 In Celtic Europe, people began to believe that magical creatures lived in the woods around them. These creatures became known as fairies. They were said to look like humans, but they posessed magical powers such as the ability to fly. Mostly, fairies' mischief was playful, but they could be unkind too.

▼ Since Victorian times (1837–1901), fairies have mostly been depicted as tiny girls with insect wings. In earlier times, they could be as tall as humans.

78 In Scandinavian folklore, the hills and mountains were inhabited by elves. Like fairies, elves could be unkind if offended. People thought they caused an irritating skin rash called elven blow, so they left offerings out for the elves to discourage any bad behavior.

◀ The *Harry Potter* stories feature a good elf called Dobby, who becomes Harry's friend.

79 In northern European folklore, hairy cannibals called trolls could sniff out humans with their large noses. In some places, trolls were believed to be giants and in others dwarves, but all trolls were evil. However, they had one fatal weakness – if a person found out a troll's name, he or she could kill the troll just by saying it.

80 **In Scottish folklore, mythical creatures called brownies helped around the house.** It was thought that these little people appeared at night to carry out helpful deeds, and disappeared before dawn. In return people left out food and drink for them. In some villages there were special flat, thin stones called brownie's stones, where offerings were left.

81 **Was there ever a race of tiny people?** In 1892, folklore expert David MacRitchie suggested that fairylore might be based on real events. Perhaps there was once a race of small people who were forced into hiding as Celtic civilizations grew rich and powerful in Scotland, around 200 BC.

▶ The story of *The Borrowers* (1952) by Mary Norton is the first in a series of novels about a race of tiny people who live beneath the floor of a house and "borrow" the things they need from humans.

Magical lands

▲ The wicked White Witch made sure it is always winter in the land of Narnia, as shown in the 2005 film *The Chronicles of Narnia: The Lion, the Witch and the Wardrobe*.

82 Children can only reach the land of Narnia through a magical wardrobe. Narnia is a fictional world inhabited by dwarves, mythical creatures and talking animals, and its ruler is a godlike lion called Aslan. This magical land was dreamt up by C. S. Lewis and first featured in his children's book *The Lion, the Witch and the Wardrobe* in 1949.

IMAGINE A LAND

1. Find a quiet place and make sure you have a pen and paper.
2. Think of a name for your imaginary land and write it down.
3. Describe what your imaginary land looks like.
4. What creatures live there? They could be fairies or unicorns, or you could invent some creatures of your own. Give them names, too.
5. Think of a password to enter your imaginary land and write it down. Keep your imaginary land secret — only share it with your best friends.

▶ Peter Pan, along with the fairy Tinkerbell and the Lost Boys, are the most well-known inhabitants of Neverland – a paradise island where people do not grow old.

83 Scottish author J. M. Barrie invented a magical children's paradise called Neverland in his play *Peter Pan*. The children who visit Neverland cannot grow older while they are there, and once grown up they cannot return to Neverland. J. M. Barrie wanted Neverland to represent the imagination of children, and to show how it is lost with adulthood.

84 The ancient Egyptians believed in the existence of a dangerous magical underworld called **Duat**. They thought that dead people had to pass through Duat to reach the afterlife, where they would live forever. There were many dangers, such as poisonous snakes and lakes of fire. To help the dead get past these dangers, each of them was given a map, a set of magic spells and protective amulets.

Anubis

85 From the 12th to 17th centuries, some Europeans believed in a magical land ruled by a Christian king, somewhere in Asia or Africa. It was believed to be full of wonders, such as the Fountain of Youth – a natural spring with the power of making the old young again. There were many expeditions to search for this land.

◀ Egyptian god Anubis was thought to help the souls of the dead enter Duat.

Magical events

86 **Eclipses were warnings of destruction.** In ancient Chinese traditions, during a solar eclipse, people believed that a dragon was devouring the Sun. To frighten the dragon away, people banged drums and made lots of noise. In 1628, an astrologer gave Pope Urban VIII a magic spell to protect him against the dangerous effects of a lunar eclipse.

▲ In astrology, eclipses of the Sun and the Moon were thought to be bad omens, or signs.

87 **In 1920, photographs of "real" fairies were printed in a British magazine.** They were taken by cousins Frances and Elsie Wright, aged 10 and 16. Author Sir Arthur Conan Doyle told the girls' story in the book *The Coming of the Fairies*, making the story known around the world. Over 50 years later, Elsie admitted that they had faked the photographs with just paper, pens and scissors.

◄ Photographs such as this, showing Elsie Wright with a "fairy," had experts fooled for years.

88 **People have reported showers of animals, all over the world.** Every year between May and July in Honduras, Central America, storms bring a rain of fish. In 1973, in Arkansas, golfers were interrupted by a shower of thousands of frogs! Experts think tornadoes may be to blame for such showers.

◀ Tornadoes passing over lakes or the sea may suck up water, making a waterspout. They might suck up animals too.

89 **In 1922, archaeologists opened the tomb of Egyptian pharaoh Tutankhamun.** Months after the tomb's opening, one of its discoverers, Lord Carnarvon, died from an infected mosquito bite. Might this death have been due to a mummy's curse? Some mummies' tombs did carry warnings, but none were ever found on Tutankhamun's.

QUIZ

1. Why did people in ancient China make noise during an eclipse?
2. Who wrote the book *The Coming of the Fairies*?
3. What did Lord Carnarvon die of?

Answers:
1. To scare away the dragon they thought was devouring the Sun 2. Sir Arthur Conan Doyle 3. Infected mosquito bite

▼ The mummy of Tutankhamun still lies in its tomb in the Valley of the Kings, Egypt, and is open for public viewing.

Superstition

90 Much of the magic from the past lives on today in the form of superstitions and customs. All cultures have their own superstitions, based on different beliefs. Some people believe in superstitions, others practice them out of habit, and some defy them on purpose to show they are not superstitious.

91 Breaking a mirror brings seven years' bad luck. This superstition comes from an ancient Roman idea that life renews itself every seven years. It was also believed that the reflected image represents the soul, and damaging it hurts the individual too. As mirrors were more commonly used in the 1500s, it became unlucky to break one.

▼ Here are some superstitions that are still alive today.

Good Luck

✿ **FOUR-LEAF CLOVERS**
Finding a four-leaf clover brings good luck.

✿ **KNOCKING ON WOOD**
To knock on wood when speaking of bad luck stops it from coming true.

✿ **PENNIES**
Finding a penny and picking it up will bring good luck for the rest of the day.

✿ **RABBIT'S FOOT**
Carrying a rabbit's foot brings good luck and protects the person from evil spirits.

✿ **CROSSING YOUR FINGERS**
Crossing your fingers wards off evil spirits and bad luck, and helps wishes come true.

Bad Luck

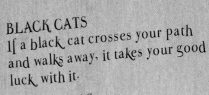

BLACK CATS
If a black cat crosses your path and walks away, it takes your good luck with it.

UMBRELLAS
Opening an umbrella indoors brings bad luck.

WALKING UNDER LADDERS
It is bad luck to walk under a leaning ladder.

MAGPIES
Seeing a lone magpie is a sign of bad luck because they stay with one mate for life.

SALT
Spilling salt is thought to cause an argument that day. To ward off bad luck, people throw a pinch of salt over their left shoulder.

▶ The 13th day of the month falls on a friday up to three times each year.

QUIZ

1. How many years bad luck is a broken mirror thought to bring?
2. How many witches were thought to meet on a Friday?
3. Why is the number four unlucky in the Far East?

Answers:
1. Seven years 2. 12, and one devil 3. The word for four sounds like the word for death

92 **Unlucky Friday 13th may come from the European belief in witchcraft.** One theory says that Friday was the day that witches held ceremonies to conduct harmful magic. It was said that 12 witches and one devil would meet each Friday, making the number 13 and Friday a doubly unlucky combination.

93 **In China and East Asia there is a superstition called tetraphobia – fear of the number four.** The number is thought to be so unlucky that multistory buildings are often missing a fourth floor. This superstition has come about because the word for four sounds similar to the word for death in several Far Eastern languages.

94 **People whose careers may involve risk and uncertainty, such as actors, may be superstitious.** There are many superstitions attached to careers in the theater. Even wishing an actor "good luck" is unlucky! Instead, it is custom to say "break a leg." Another theater superstition says that a stage should never be left dark. A light, called a "ghost light," is left on after a performance to keep the ghosts of past performers content.

▶ Lady Macbeth is the wicked wife in Shakespeare's famous play *Macbeth*. Actors consider it unlucky to speak the name of the play, instead calling it "the Scottish Play."

Illusionist magic

95 Illusionist magic involves trickery and skill rather than supernatural powers. It is practiced by performance magicians to entertain audiences. These magicians do not pretend to have magical powers, but use their talents to create the illusion of magic.

▲ A classic illusionist's trick is to "saw a person in half." During Italian magician Gaetano Trigginao's show *Tablo*, a man is seemingly cut in two.

96 Stage magicians perform magic tricks in theaters and at parties. Typical stage tricks include making objects appear apparently from nowhere, such as pulling a coin from a person's ear. Or the magician might transform objects, for example, turning a white handkerchief red.

▲ A well-known stage trick involves pulling a rabbit out of a hat.

97 Escapology is the art of escaping from restraints such as ropes, chains and handcuffs in death-defying stunts. In the early 1900s, American Harry Houdini made daring escapes using just skill and flexibility. He learned how to pick locks, and he could dislocate his shoulders to narrow his body to help him escape.

▼ Escapologist Harry Houdini became known as "The Handcuff King" because of his incredible ability to free himself.

98 In the 21st century, escapology has given way to endurance art. Endurance artists such as David Blaine perform stunts that rely on extraordinary physical stamina and mental training. Endurance stunts seem to bend the normal laws of nature.

99 Mentalist magicians create the illusion that they have psychic powers, such as the ability to mind-read. Often, they reveal the techniques they use, such as hypnosis, suggestion and reading body language, to achieve the illusion. This can be even more amazing to the audience than their claims of psychic powers.

100 Magicians have exposed fakes. Harry Houdini exposed the methods that psychics used to convince people that they could "speak" to the dead. In recent times, American magician and supernatural skeptic James Randi has exposed similar tricksters.

▲ In 2000, at New York City's Times Square, David Blaine stood inside a block of ice for 63 hours. Among his other amazing feats, Blaine stood for 35 hours upon a pole 98 feet (30m) high.

Glossary

alchemy: a medieval chemical science and speculative philosophy aiming to change metals into gold, discover a universal cure for disease, and discover a means of indefinitely prolonging life

amulet: a charm (as an ornament) often inscribed with a magic incantation or symbol to aid the wearer or protect against evil (as disease or witchcraft)

astrologer: a person who practices the divination of the supposed influences of the stars and planets on human affairs

divination: the art or practice that seeks to foresee or foretell future events or discover hidden knowledge usually by the interpretation of omens or by the aid of supernatural powers

folklore: an often unsupported notion, story, or saying that is widely circulated

hallucinogenic: a substance that induces hallucinations, the perception of objects with no or distorted reality

horoscope: an astrological forecast

levitation: the act or process of rising or lifting a person or thing by means held to be supernatural

narwhal: an arctic ocean mammal about 20 feet (6 m) long with the male having a long, twisted ivory tusk

oracle: a person (as a priestess of ancient Greece) through whom a deity is believed to speak

palmistry: the art or practice of reading a person's character or future from the lines on the hands

pendulum: a weighted stick that swings back and forth at a regular rate

shaman: a priest or priestess who uses magic for the purpose of curing the sick, divining the hidden, and controlling events

supernatural: of or relating to an order of existence beyond the visible observable universe

tasseographer: a person who practices divination by reading the arrangement of leaves of tea

For More Information

Books

Haughton, Brian. *History's Mysteries.* Wayne, NJ: New Page Books, 2010.

Rice, Dona Herweck. *Unsolved: History's Mysteries.* Huntington Beach, CA: Teacher Created Materials, 2013.

Sherman, Patrice. *The Unusual History of Magic.* Mankato, MN: Capstone, 2011.

Websites

History of Magic
http://magictricksforkids.org/category/history-of-magic/
Read articles about some famous magicians.

Magic and Magicians
http://www.magicandmagicians.com/
Learn about magic and some of history's greatest magicians.

Mysterynet's Kids Mysteries
http://kids.mysterynet.com/
Try to solve some mysterious cases, and play other games, too!

Index